Flicks

&

Phrases

The Ultimate Movie Quote Trivia Game
Volume I

By

Peter David Orr

BEACHFRONT PRESS

First Edition – February 2024

Flicks & Phrases: The Ultimate Movie Quote Trivia Game, Vol. 1:

Peter David Orr

ISBN 979-887733647-6

Printed in the United States of America

HOW TO PLAY

Challenge yourself. Go head-to-head. Play in small or large groups with friends and family. This trivia game in book form is packed with 90 of the most memorable movie quotes.

There are many ways to play. Just agree to the rules ahead of time and go for it. Alternatively, use the following example:

- Divide participants into **two teams**.
- **Team A** has the book.
- Someone designated as "Team Captain" of **Team A** reads the quote out loud for **Team B**.
- **Team B** has **30 seconds** to discuss. One person on **Team B**, designated as "Team Captain," then gives the final answer (The correct answer has a **checkmark** next to it. It is one of the 4 possible answer choices found directly below the quote).
- If **Team B** gives the correct answer on the first try, they get **10 points,** and the book is now passed to **Team B's** Captain to repeat the process.
- If **Team B** answers incorrectly, they get a second chance.
- **Team A's** Captain reads the four multiple-choice answers and **Team B** has ten seconds to discuss and debate the choices.
- If **Team B's** Captain gives the correct answer, **Team B** gets **5 points,** after which the book is passed to **Team A's** Captain, and the previously established pattern is followed.
- No **"stealing"** of questions is allowed unless both teams agree to the process and points before the game begins.

-1-

Quote 1: "Frankly, my dear, I don't give a damn."

Quote 2: "After all, tomorrow is another day!"

A. Casablanca (1942)
B. Psycho (1960)
C. Gone with the Wind (1939) ☑
D. 12 Angry Men (1957)

-2-

Quote 1: "A boy's best friend is his mother."

Quote 2: " I couldn't do that. Who would look after her? The fire in her fireplace would go out. It would be cold and damp up there like a grave."

A. The Bates Hotel (1960)

B. North by Northwest (1959)

C. To Kill a Mockingbird (1962)

D. Psycho (1960) ☑

$$-3-$$

Quote 1: "Here's looking at you, kid."

Quote 2: "Louis, I think this is the beginning of
a beautiful friendship."

A. Gone with the Wind (1939)

B. Casablanca (1942) ☑

C. Psycho (1960)

D. North by Northwest (1959)

-4-

Quote 1: Quintus Arrius: Now listen to me, all of you. You are all condemned men. We keep you alive to serve this ship. So row well, and live.

Quote 2: "The race is not over when one crosses the line."

A. Roman Holiday (1953)

B. The Bridge on the River Kwai (1957)

C. Lawrence of Arabia (1962)

D. Ben-Hur (1959) ☑

-5-

Quote 1: "It's always difficult to keep personal prejudice out of a thing like this."

Quote 2: "Brother, I've seen all kinds of dishonesty in my day, but this little display takes the cake. Y'all come in here with your hearts bleedin' all over the floor about slum kids and injustice, you listen to some fairy tales... Suddenly, you start gettin' through to some of these old ladies. Well, you're not getting through to me, I've had enough.

A. 12 Angry Men (1957) ☑

B. North by Northwest (1959)

C. The Bridge on the River Kwai (1957)

D. Vertigo (1958)

-6-

Quote 1: "That's funny, that plane's dustin' crops where there ain't no crops."

Quote 2: "I've got a job, a secretary, a mother, two ex-wives, and several bartenders that depend upon me, and I don't intend to disappoint them all by getting myself 'slightly' killed."

A. Lawrence of Arabia (1962)

B. Vertigo (1958)

C. North by Northwest (1959) ☑

D. Of Mice and Men (1937)

-7-

Quote: "You make me sick with your heroics! There's a stench of death about you. You carry it in your pack like the plague."

Quote 2: "Do not speak to me of rules. This is war! This is not a game of cricket!"

A. The Bridge on the River Kwai (1957) ☑

B. North by Northwest (1959)

C. Ben-Hur (1959)

D. Lawrence of Arabia (1962)

-8-

Quote 1: "Look at that! Look how she moves. It's like Jell-O on springs."

Quote 2:

Jerry : But you don't understand, Osgood! Ohh...

[Jerry finally gives up and pulls off his wig]

Jerry : I'm a man!

Osgood : [shrugs] Well, nobody's perfect!

A. Roman Holiday (1953)

B. The Graduate (1967)

C. Dude Looks Like a Lady (1978)

D. Some Like It Hot (1959) ☑

-9-

Quote 1: "I killed two people. One was... yesterday? He was just a boy and I led him into quicksand. The other was...well, before Aqaba. I had to execute him with my pistol, and there was something about it that I didn't like."

Quote 2: "My lord, I think... I think your book is right. 'The desert is an ocean in which no oar is dipped' and on this ocean the Bedu go where they please and strike where they please."

A. The Graduate (1967)

B. Lawrence of Arabia (1962) ☑

C. Roman Holiday (1953)

D. The Bridge on the River Kwai (1957)

-10-

Quote 1: "You got the bullets in the gun. You're gonna be a big man in this neighborhood."

Quote 2:

Jim Stark: I don't know what to do anymore. Except maybe die.

A. Rebel Without a Cause (1955) ☑

B. West Side Story (1961)

C. Roman Holiday (1953)

D. Iron Man (1947)

-11-

Quote: "You never really understand a person until you consider things from his point of view."

Quote 2:

Scout: "Atticus, he was real nice."

Atticus: "Most people are, Scout, when you finally see them."

    A. Rebel Without a Cause (1955)

    B. Ben-Hur (1959)

    C. Vertigo (1958)

    D. To Kill a Mockingbird (1962) ☑

-12-

Quote 1: "Only one is a wanderer; two together are always going somewhere."

Quote 2: "I was safe when you found me. There was nothing that you could prove. When I saw you again, I couldn't run away. I loved you so. I walked into danger, let you change me because I loved you and you needed me."

A. Ben-Hur (1959)

B. The Graduate (1967)

C. Vertigo (1958) ☑

D. A Wayward Life (1930)

-13-

Quote: "When the Lord closes a door, somewhere He opens a window.

Quote 2: "Climb every mountain, ford every stream, follow every rainbow, till you find your dream."

A. Roman Holiday (1953)

B. The Family von Trapp (1943)

C. The Sound of Music (1965) ☑

D. The Hills Have Eyes (1970)

-14-

Quote 1: "That's the way it crumbles... cookie-wise."

Quote 2:

C.C. Baxter: The mirror... it's broken.

Fran Kubelik: Yes, I know. I like it that way. Makes me look the way I feel.

A. The Apartment (1960) ☑

B. The Seven Year Itch (1955)

C. Roman Holiday (1953)

D. The Graduate (1967)

-15-

Quote 1: "I have to leave you now. I'm going to that corner there and turn. You must stay in the car and drive away. Promise not to watch me go beyond the corner. Just drive away and leave me as I leave you."

Quote 2: "I know. I'll hide in the dark until it's morning. Then I'll go home."

A. The Seven Year Itch (1955)

B. The Graduate (1967)

C. The Long Journey Home (1944)

D. Roman Holiday (1953) ☑

-16-

Quote 1: "You could always tell what kind of a person a man thinks you are by the earrings he gives you. I must say, the mind reels."

Quote 2: "It's useful being top banana in the shock department."

A. The Seven Year Itch (1955)

B. Second Banana (1942)

C. A Streetcar Named Desire (1951)

D. Breakfast at Tiffany's (1961) ☑

-17-

Quote 1: "Mrs. Robinson, you're trying to seduce me. Aren't you?"

Quote 2: "Listen to me. What happened between Mrs. Robinson and me was nothing. It didn't mean anything. We might just as well have been shaking hands."

A. The Seven Year Itch (1955)

B. The Apartment (1960)

C. The Graduate (1967) ☑

D. The Swiss Family Robinson (1960)

-18-

Quote 1: "I have always depended on the kindness of strangers."

Quote 2: "I want to kiss you just once, softly and sweetly on your mouth!"

A. A Streetcar Named Desire (1951) ☑

B. The Seven Year Itch (1955)

C. The Apartment (1960)

D. Casablanca (1942)

-19-

Quote 1: "I feel pretty, oh so pretty!"

Quote 2: [singing] Here come the Jets, like a bat out of hell - Someone gets in our way, someone don't feel so well.

A. Rebel Without a Cause (1955)

B. West Side Story (1961) ☑

C. Benny and the Jets (1961)

D. Breakfast at Tiffany's (1961)

-20-

Quote 1:

The Girl: Oo! Do you feel the breeze from the subway? Isn't it delicious!

Richard Sherman: It sort of cools the ankles, doesn't it?

Quote 2: "When it gets hot like this, you know what I do? I keep my undies in the icebox!"

A. The Seven Year Itch (1955) ☑

B. West Side Story (1961)

C. Rebel Without a Cause (1955)

D. The Graduate (1967)

-21-

Quote 1: "I find your lack of faith disturbing."

Quote 2: "Look, Your Worshipfulness, let's get one thing straight. I take orders from just one person: me."

A. Benny and the Jets (1961)

B. Star Wars (1977) ☑

C. The Godfather (1972)

D. Indiana Jones: The Last Crusade (1999)

-22-

Quote 1: "Leave the gun, take the cannoli."

Quote 2: What's the matter with you? Is this what you've become, a Hollywood finocchio who cries like a woman? "Oh, what do I do? What do I do?" What is that nonsense? Ridiculous!

A. Down and Out in Beverly Hills (1986)

B. The Godfather (1972) ☑

C. The Godfather II (1980)

D. Rocky (1976)

-23-

Quote 1: "We're all crazy, but I'm trying to save you and me."

Quote 2: They was giving me ten thousand watts a day, you know, and I'm hot to trot! The next woman takes me on's gonna light up like a pinball machine and pay off in silver dollars!

A. The Sting (1973)

B. One Flew Over the Cuckoo's Nest (1975) ☑

C. A Clockwork Orange (1971)

D. Apocalypse Now (1979)

-24-

Quote 1: "I just want to prove that I'm not another bum from the neighborhood."

Quote 2:

Mickey: "Women weaken legs!"

A. Rocky II (1980)

B. Rocky (1976) ☑

C. The Godfather (1972)

D. Chinatown (1974)

Quote 1: "It's funny how the colors of the real world only seem really real when you viddy them on the screen."

Quote 2: "There was me, that is Alex, and my three droogs, that is Pete, Georgie, and Dim, and we sat in the Korova Milkbar trying to make up our rassoodocks what to do with the evening."

A. The Deer Hunter (1978)

B. Apocalypse Now (1979)

C. A Clockwork Orange (1971) ☑

D. Monty Python and the Holy Grail (1975)

-26-

Quote 1: "You're gonna need a bigger boat."

Quote 2: "Y'know the thing about a shark, he's got... lifeless eyes, black eyes, like a doll's eyes."

A. The Poseidon Adventures (1972)

B. Jaws (1975) ☑

C. Jaws II (1978)

D. Jaws: The Revenge (1987)

-27-

Quote 1: "I watched a snail crawl along the edge of a straight razor. That's my dream; that's my nightmare. Crawling, slithering, along the edge of a straight razor... and surviving."

Quote 2: "I like the smell of napalm in the morning. It smells like... victory."

A. The Deer Hunter (1978)

B. Apocalypse Now (1979) ☑

C. Platoon (1986)

D. Coming Home (1978)

-28-

Quote 1: Sir Galahad: "Look, it's my duty as a knight to sample as much peril as I can."

Quote 2: "Listen, strange women lyin' in ponds distributin' swords is no basis for a system of government. Supreme executive power derives from a mandate from the masses, not from some farcical aquatic ceremony."

A. The Court Jester (1955)

B. A Knight's Tale (2001)

C. Monty Python and the Holy Grail (1975) ☑

D. Star Wars (1977)

-29-

Quote 1: "What the hell else are you gonna do with your money if you can't get candy bars?"

Quote 2:

Doyle Lonnegan: Your boss is quite a card player, Mr. Kelly; how does he do it?

Johnny Hooker: He cheats.

A. Aces High (1945)

B. The Sting (1973) ☑

C. The Great Train Robbery (1957)

D. The Hustler (1961)

-30-

Quote 1: "A relationship, I think, is like a shark. You know? It has to constantly move forward or it dies."

Quote 2: "I feel that life is divided into the horrible and the miserable. That's the two categories. The horrible are like, I don't know, terminal cases, you know, and blind people, crippled. I don't know how they get through life. It's amazing to me. And the miserable is everyone else. So you should be thankful that you're miserable, because that's very lucky, to be miserable."

A. Jaws (1972)

B. Annie Hall (1977) ☑

C. The Sting (1973)

D. For the Love of Misery (1950)

-31-

Quote 1: "You're a very nosy fellow, kitty cat."

Quote 2: "Isn't that something? Middle of a drought and the water commissioner drowns. Only in L.A."

A. Chinatown (1974) ☑

B. Cat on a Hot Tin Roof (1958)

C. Cat Woman (1977)

D. L.A. Story (1981)

-32-

Quote 1: "This is this. This ain't somethin' else. This is this."

Quote 2: "I'm thinking about the deer. Going to 'Nam. I like the trees, you know? I like the way that the trees are on mountains, all the different... the way the trees are."

A. The Killing of the Sacred Deer (1979)

B. The Yearling (1946)

C. The Deer Hunter (1978) ☑

D. The White Reindeer (1952)

-33-

Quote 1: "It's too good to be true. He's 6' 4", has black hair, blue eyes, doesn't drink, doesn't smoke, and tells the truth."

Quote 2: "Easy, miss. I've got you...You - you've got me? Who's got you?

A. Superman (1978) ☑

B. Superman II (1980)

C. Dirty Dancing (1983)

D. Volcano (1942)

-34-

Quote 1: "I know this sounds crazy, but ever since yesterday on the road, I've been seeing this shape. Shaving cream, pillows... Dammit! I know this. I know what this is! This means something. This is important."

Quote 2:
Roy Neary: "I guess you've noticed something a little strange with Dad. It's okay, though. I'm still Dad.

A. Back to the Future (1985)

B. Ghostbusters (1984)

C. Close Encounters of the Third Kind (1977) ☑

D. Dawn of the Dead (1956)

-35-

Quote 1: "It's all on account of that goddamn saw. You ruined the door."

Quote 2: "The film which you are about to see is an account of the tragedy which befell a group of five youths, in particular Sally Hardesty and her invalid brother, Franklin. It is all the more tragic in that they were young."

A. The Horror of Frankenstein (1971)

B. Dawn of the Dead (1956)

C. Dorian Gray (1945)

D. The Texas Chain Saw Massacre (1974) ☑

-36-

Quote 1: "The way I see it, if you're gonna build a time machine into a car, why not do it with some style?"

Quote 2: "If my calculations are correct, when this baby hits 88 miles per hour, you're gonna see some serious sh*t."

A. Back to the Future (1985) ☑

B. Back to the Future II (1989)

C. Back to the Future III (1990)

D. The Time Machine (1988)

-37-

Quote 1: "Does Barry Manilow know that you raid his wardrobe?"

Quote 2: "We're all pretty bizarre. Some of us are just better at hiding it, that's all."

A. Ocean's Eleven (2002)

B. Sixteen Candles (1984)

C. The Breakfast Club (1985) ☑

D. Never Been Kissed (1999)

-38-

Quote 1:

Janine Melnitz: Do you believe in UFOs, astral projections, mental telepathy, ESP, clairvoyance, spirit photography, telekinetic movement, full trance mediums, the Loch Ness monster, and the theory of Atlantis?

Winston Zeddemore: Ah, if there's a steady paycheck in it, I'll believe anything you say.

Quote 2:

Dr. Peter Venkman: This city is headed for a disaster of biblical proportions.

    A. The Frighteners (1996)

    B. Weird Science (1985)

    C. Ghostbusters (1984) ☑

    D. Shaun of the Dead (2002)

-39-

Quote 1: "No, I am your father."

Quote 2: "Do or do not. There is no try."

A. Star Wars (1977)

B. The Empire Strikes Back (1980) ☑

C. Return of the Jedi (1983)

D. The Phantom Menace (1999)

-40-

Quote 1: "Snakes. Why'd it have to be snakes?"

Quote 2: "It's not the years, honey. It's the mileage."

A. Indiana Jones and the Temple of Doon (1984)

B. Raiders of the Lost Ark (1981) ☑

C. Indiana Jones and the Last Crusade (1989)

D. Snakes on a Plane (2008)

-41-

Quote 1: "Life moves pretty fast. If you don't stop and look around once in a while, you could miss it."

Quote 2: "It is his fault he didn't lock the garage."

A. Ferris Bueller's Day Off (1986) ☑

B. Sixteen Candles (1984)

C. Never Been Kissed (1999)

D. The Breakfast Club (1985)

-42-

Quote 1: "Here's Johnny!"

Quote 2: "All work and no play makes Jack a dull boy."

A. The Little Shop of Horrors (1960)

B. The Shining (1980) ☑

C. One Flew Over the Cuckoo's Nest (1975)

D. The Witches of Eastwick (1985)

-43-

Quote 1: "I've seen things you people wouldn't believe."

Quote 2: "It's too bad she won't live. But then again, who does?"

A. Star Wars (1977)

B. The Departed (2006)

C. Blade Runner (1982) ☑

D. The Two Jakes (1990)

-44-

Quote 1: "I feel the need... the need for speed."

Quote 2: "You can be my wingman anytime."

A. Risky Business (1983)

B. Top Gun (1986) ☑

C. All the Right Moves (1983)

D. Mission: Impossible (1996)

-45-

Quote 1: "Hello. My name is Inigo Montoya. You killed my father. Prepare to die."

Quote 2: "You keep using that word. I do not think it means what you think it means."

A. Mission: Impossible (1996)

B. Breakaway (1977)

C. The Forgotten Man (1945)

D. The Princess Bride (1987) ☑

-46-

Quote 1: "...you have me at a loss. You know my name but who are you? Just another American who saw too many movies as a child? Another orphan of a bankrupt culture who thinks he's John Wayne? Rambo? Marshal Dillon?"

Quote 2: "Welcome to the party, pal!"

A. Die Hard II (1990)
B. Die Hard With a Vengeance (1995)
C. Die Hard (1988) ☑
D. Live Free of Die Hard (2007)

-47-

Quote 1: " But choose wisely, for while the true Grail will bring you life, the false Grail will take it from you."

Quote 2: "...goose-stepping morons like yourself should try *reading* books instead of *burning* them!"

A. Indiana Jones and the Last Crusade (1989) ☑
B. Indiana Jones and the Temple of Doon (1984)
C. Raiders of the Lost Ark (1981)
D. The Knight's Curse (1967)

-48-

Quote 1: "One, two, Freddy's coming for you..."

Quote 2: "Whatever you do, don't fall asleep."

    A. Freddy Kruger (1979)
    B. Be Steady Freddy (1956)
    C. A Nightmare on Elm Street (1984) ☑
    D. Wide Awake (1969)

-49-

Quote 1: "Wax on, wax off."

Quote 2: "Sweep the leg."

    A. Car Wash (1976)
    B. Rocky (1976)
    C. Dirty Dancing (1987)
    D. The Karate Kid (1984) ☑

-50-

Quote 1: "I'll be back."

Quote 2: "Come with me if you want to live."

- A. Commando (1985)
- B. The Terminator (1984) ☑
- C. Terminator II: Judgement Day (1991)
- D. Terminator III: Rise of the Machines (2003)

-51-

Quote 1: "Nobody puts Baby in a corner."

Quote 2: "Look, spaghetti arms. This is my dance space. This is your dance space. I don't go into yours, you don't go into mine. You gotta hold the frame."

A. Road House (1989)
B. The Outsiders (1983)
C. Point Break (1991)
D. Dirty Dancing (1987) ☑

-52-

Quote 1: "What you have to understand is, four days ago he was only my brother in name. And this morning we had pancakes."

Quote 2: "Raymond: Uh oh fart. Uh oh fart. Charlie: Did you fart, Ray?"

A. Breakfast at Tiffany's (1961)
B. Rain Man (1988) ☑
C. Everyone Loves Raymond (1999)
D. Charlie and Raymond's Big Adventure (1988)

-53-

Quote 1: "Let's turn on the juice and see what shakes loose."

Quote 2: "I'm a ghost with the most, babe."

A. Ghostbusters (1984)
B. Beetlejuice (1988) ☑
C. The Frightening (1970)
D. Edward Scissorhands (1990)

-54-

Quote 1: "I've got to get into this dude's pelt and crawl around for a few days."

Quote 2: "Cinderella story. Outta nowhere. A former greenskeeper, now, about to become the Masters champion."

A. The Outing (1977)
B. Billy Madison (2002)
C. The Green Jacket (1971)
D. Caddyshack (1980) ☑

-55-

Quote 1: "It's only after we've lost everything that we're free to do anything."

Quote 2: "You are the all-singing, all-dancing crap of the world."

A. Donnie Darko (2001)
B. Taxi Driver (1975)
C. Fight Club (1999) ☑
D. Beetlejuice (1988)

-56-

Quote 1: "Say 'what' again! I dare you; I double dare you!"

Quote 2: "Royale with Cheese."

A. Pulp Fiction (1994) ☑
B. The Pin Up Girl (1960)
C. A Christmas Story (1983)
D. Planes, Trains, and Automobiles (1987)

-57-

Quote 1: "Get busy living or get busy dying."

Quote 2: "Hope is a good thing, maybe the best of things, and no good thing ever dies."

A. The Good Shepherd (1979)
B. The Shawshank Redemption (1994) ☑
C. The Best of Things (1999)
D. The Green Mile (1999)

-58-

Quote 1: "Life is like a box of chocolates; you never know what you're gonna get."

Quote 2: "Jenny and me was like peas and carrots."

A. Forrest Gump (1994) ☑
B. Big (1988)
C. Toy Story (1995)
D. Nothing in Common (1986)

-59-

Quote 1: "This is your last chance. After this, there is no turning back. You take the blue pill - the story ends, you wake up in your bed and believe whatever you want to believe. You take the red pill - you stay in Wonderland, and I show you how deep the rabbit hole goes."

Quote 2:
Spoon boy: Then you'll see that it is not the spoon that bends, it is only yourself.

A. The Matrix (1999) ☑
B. The Matrix Reloaded (2003)
C. The Matrix Revolutions (2003)
D. The Matrix Revelations (2003)

-60-

Quote 1: "I'm the king of the world!"

Quote 2: "Jack, I want you to draw me like one of your French girls."

A. Jack and the Beanstalk (1955)
B. King of the World (1957)
C. Titanic (1997) ☑
D. The Parisian (1959)

-61-

Quote 1: "Life finds a way."

Quote 2: God creates dinosaurs. God destroys dinosaurs. God creates man. Man destroys God. Man creates dinosaurs.

A. The Lost World: Jurassic Park (1997)
B. Jurassic Park (1993) ☑
C. Jurassic Park III (2001)
D. Journey to the Center of the Earth (1961)

-62-

Quote 1: "I'm the Dude. So that's what you call me. You know, that or, uh, His Dudeness, or uh, Duder, or El Duderino if you're not into the whole brevity thing."

Quote 2: "The Dude abides. I don't know about you but I take comfort in that. It's good knowin' he's out there. The Dude. Takin' 'er easy for all us sinners."

A. The Big Lebowski (1998) ☑
B. Fear & Loathing In Las Vegas (1996)
C. Kiss Kiss Bang Bang (1997)
D. The Dude (1998)

-63-

Quote 1: "I ate his liver with some fava beans and a nice Chianti."

Quote 2: "It rubs the lotion on its skin or else it gets the hose again."

A. Misery (1990)
B. Hannibal (2001)
C. Primal Fear (1996)
D. The Silence of the Lambs (1991) ☑

-64-

Quote 1: "So you're telling me there's a chance."

Quote 2: "Mock... yeah! Ing... yeah! Bird... yeah!"

    A. Ace Ventura: Pet Detective (1994)
    B. Dumb and Dumber (1994) ☑
    C. The Mask (1992)
    D. Liar Liar (1997)

-65-

Quote 1: "Hakuna Matata!"

Quote 2:

Timon: Pumbaa, with you, everything's gas.

    A. Pumbaa (1994)
    B. Hakuna Matata (1994)
    C. The Circle of Life (1994)
    D. The Lion King (1994) ☑

-66-

Quote 1: "They may take our lives, but they'll never take our freedom!"

Quote 2: "Every man dies, not every man really lives."

A. Lionheart (1989)
B. Robert the Bruce (1977)
C. Braveheart (1995) ☑
D. Edward Longshanks (1995)

-67-

Quote 1: "To infinity and beyond!"

Quote 2: "You are a toy!"

A. Toy Story (1995) ☑
B. Toy Story II (1999)
C. Toy Story III (2010)
D. Toy Story IV (2019)

-68-

Quote 1: "Funny how? Like I'm a clown, I amuse you?"

Quote 2: "As far back as I can remember, I always wanted to be a gangster."

A. The Godfather (1972)
B. The Godfather – Part 2 (1974)
C. Goodfellas (1990) ☑
D. Scarface (1983)

-69-

Quote 1: "I see dead people."

Quote 2: "I'm ready to communicate with the dead."

A. The Fifth Sense (1999)
B. The Sixth Sense (1999) ☑
C. Seven (1999)
D. The Walking Dead (1955)

-70-

Quote 1: "Good morning. And in case I don't see ya...good afternoon, good evening, and good night!"

Quote 2: "We accept the reality of the world with which we're presented."

A. The Truman Show (1998) ☑
B. Vanilla Sky (2001)
C. EdTV (1999)
D. Pleasantville (1998)

-71-

Quote 1: "What if there is no tomorrow? There wasn't one today."

Quote 2: "I'm not going to live by their rules anymore."

A. Die Another Day (1995)
B. Charlie's Rules (1970)
C. Tomorrow Never Dies (1998)
D. Groundhog Day (1993) ☑

-72-

Quote 1: "You can't handle the truth!"

Quote 2: "Son, we live in a world that has walls, and those walls have to be guarded by men with guns. Who's gonna do it? You? You, Lt. Weinberg? I have a greater responsibility than you could possibly fathom."

A. Presumed Innocent (1990)
B. Runaway Jury (2003)
C. L.A. Confidential (1997).
D. A Few Good Men (1992) ☑

-73-

Quote 1: Cher: Ugh, as if!

Quote 2: "It does not say RSVP on the Statue of Liberty."

A. She's All That (1999)
B. Mean Girls (2004)
C. Can't Hardly Wait (1998)
D. Clueless (1995) ☑

-74-

Quote 1:

Captain Miller: I'm a schoolteacher. I teach English composition... in this little town called Adley, Pennsylvania. The last eleven years, I've been at Thomas Alva Edison High School. I was a coach of the baseball team in the springtime. Back home, I tell people what I do for a living, and they think well, now that figures. But over here, it's a big, a big mystery.

Quote 2: "This Ryan better be worth it. He'd better go home, cure some disease, or invent a longer-lasting light bulb or something."

A. A Bridge too Far (1968)
B. Wind Talkers (2009)
C. Saving Private Ryan (1998) ☑
D. Ryan's Song (1977)

-75-

Quote 1:

Maximus: You would fight me?

Commodus: Why not? Do you think I am afraid?

Maximus: I think you've been afraid all your life.

Quote 2: Hold the line! Stay with me! If you find yourself alone, riding in the green fields with the sun on your face, do not be troubled. For you are in Elysium, and you're already dead!

A. Gladiator (2000) ☑
B. Troy (2004)
C. Spartacus (1960)
D. The Eagle (2011)

-76-

Quote 1: "When the chips are down, these... these civilized people, they'll eat each other. See, I'm not a monster. I'm just ahead of the curve.

Quote 2: "You either die a hero, or you live long enough to see yourself become the villain."

A. Batman (1989)
B. Batman Returns (1992)
C. Batman Forever (1996)
D. The Dark Knight (2008) ☑

-77-

Quote 1: "One ring to rule them all."

Quote 2: "You shall not pass!"

    A. The Hobbit: An Unexpected Journey (2012)
    B. The Lord of the Rings: The Fellowship of the Ring (2001) ☑
    C. The Lord of the Rings: The Return of the King (2003)
    D. The Lord of the Rings: The Two Towers (2002)

-78-

Quote 1: "What is the most resilient parasite? Bacteria? A virus? An intestinal worm? An idea. Resilient... highly contagious. Once an idea has taken hold of the brain it's almost impossible to eradicate."

Quote 2: "You mustn't be afraid to dream a little bigger, darling. [Pulls out a grenade launcher]."

A. The Mind Meld (1968)
B. Hot Fuzz (2007)
C. Inception (2010) ☑
D. Eternal Sunshine of the Spotless Mind (1999)

-79-

Quote 1: "You know, you really don't need a forensics team to get to the bottom of this. If you guys were the inventors of Facebook, you'd have invented Facebook."

Quote 2: "A million dollars isn't cool. You know what's cool? A billion dollars."

A. Vanilla Sky (2001)
B. Inception (2010)
C. The Social Network (2010) ☑
D. The Minority Report (2008)

-80-

Quote 1:

Jake Sully: Everything is backwards now, like out there is the true world, and in here is the dream.

Quote 2: "I'd like to talk to you about a fresh start on a new world."

A. Inception (2010)
B. Avatar (2009) ☑
C. Pandora's Box (1977)
D. Mind Games (1983)

-81-

Quote 1:

Anna: Olaf! You're melting!

Olaf: Some people are worth melting for.

Quote 2: "Do you want to build a snowman?"

A. Frozen (2013) ☑
B. The Little Mermaid (1989)
C. Once Upon a Snowman (1999)
D. Enchanted (2007)

-82-

Quote 1: "Keep your hands off my lobby boy!"

Quote 2: "There are still faint glimmers of civilization left in this barbaric slaughterhouse that was once known as humanity."

A. The Grand Vienna Hotel (2000)
B. The Grand Berlin Hotel (2012)
C. Home Alone (1992)
D. The Grand Budapest Hotel (2014) ☑

-83-

Quote 1: "Here's to the fools who dream."

Quote 2: "City of stars, are you shining just for me?"

    A. L.A. Story (1996)
    B. La La Land (2016) ☑
    C. To Live and Die in Las Vegas (1990)
    D. La Bamba (1987)

-84-

Quote 1: "The chain in those handcuffs is high-tensile steel. It'd take you ten minutes to hack through it with this. Now, if you're lucky, you could hack through your ankle in five minutes. Go.

Quote 2: Look. Any longer out on that road and I'm one of them, you know? A terminal crazy... only I got a bronze badge to say I'm one of the good guys.

    A. Mad Max (1979) ☑
    B. The Road Warrior (1981)
    C. Mad Max: Beyond Thunderdome (1985)
    D. Mad Max: Fury Road (2015)

Quote 1:
John Coffey: He kill them wi' their love. Wi' their love fo' each other. That's how it is, every day, all over the world.

Quote 2: "You know, I fell asleep this afternoon and had me a dream. I dreamed about Del's mouse...I dreamed he got down to that place Boss Howell talked about, that Mouseville place."

A. The Green Mile (1999) ☑
B. Forrest Gump (1994)
C. The Shawshank Redemption (1994)
D. The Mouse House (2003)

-86-

Quote 1: "Love is the one thing we're capable of perceiving that transcends time and space."

Quote 2: "Do not go gentle into that good night."

A. Arrival (2016)
B. 2001: A Space Odyssey (1968)
C. Interstellar (2014) ☑
D. The Martian (2014)

-87-

Quote 1: "I could die right now, Clem. I'm just... happy. I've never felt that before."

Quote 2: "Blessed are the forgetful, for they get the better even of their blunders."

A. Punch Drunk Love (2002)
B. Being John Malkovich (1999)
C. Eternal Sunshine of the Spotless Mind (2004)
   ☑
D. 500 Days of Summer (2009)

-88-

Quote 1: "I'm the guy who does his job. You must be the other guy."

Quote 2: "What are you waiting for? Get back on your feet. You're a police officer."

A. Stranger Than Fiction (2006)
B. The Departed (2006) ☑
C. American Gangster (2007)
D. Mystic River (2003)

-89-

Quote 1:

Nash, speaking to Alicia: I have made the most important discovery of my career - the most important discovery of my life. It is only in the mysterious equations of love that any logic or reasons can be found. I am only here tonight because of you. You are the only reason I am. You are all my reasons.

Quote 2:

"I still see things that are not here. I just choose not to acknowledge them. Like a diet of the mind, I just choose not to indulge certain appetites; like my appetite for patterns; perhaps my appetite to imagine and to dream."

    A. A Beautiful Mind (2001)
    B. A Walk to Remember (2001)
    C. The Professor and the Madman (2019)
    D. The Imitation Game (2014)

-90-

Quote 1: "Wakanda forever!"

Quote 2: "It's hard for a good man to be a king."

    A. The Lion King 2: Simba's Pride (2012)
    B. The Lion King 3: Hakuna Matata (2019)
    C. Black Panther (2018) ☑
    D. The Jungle Book (1967)